D0305603

ANIMALS HEAD TO HEAD

Elephant
VS.
Rhinoceros

This book is dedicated to the memory of Lucy Owen,
who really cared about this series.

ISABEL THOMAS

www.raintreepublishers.co.uk

Visit our website to find out more information about **Raintree** books.

To order:

☎ Phone 44 (0) 1865 888112

🖹 Send a fax to 44 (0) 1865 314091

🖥 Visit the Raintree bookshop at **www.raintreepublishers.co.uk** to browse our catalogue and order online.

First published in Great Britain by Raintree,
Halley Court, Jordan Hill, Oxford OX2 8EJ,
part of Harcourt Education.
Raintree is a registered trademark
of Harcourt Education Ltd.

Editorial: Dan Nunn and Katie Shepherd
Design: Victoria Bevan   1687397
and Bridge Creative Services Ltd
Picture Research: Hannah Taylor
and Rebecca Sodergren
Production: Duncan Gilbert

Originated by Chroma Graphics Pte. Ltd
Printed and bound in China by
South China Printing Company

10 digit ISBN 1 406 20329 7
13 digit ISBN 978 1 406 20329 5

10 09 08 07 06
10 9 8 7 6 5 4 3 2 1

**British Library Cataloguing in
Publication Data**
Thomas, Isabel, 1980–
  Elephant vs. rhino. – (Animals head to head)
  1. Rhinoceroses – Juvenile literature
  2. Elephants – Africa – Juvenile literature
  3. Animal fighting – Juvenile literature
  4. Predation (Biology) – Juvenile literature
  I. Title
  599.6′681566
A full catalogue record for this book is available
from the British Library.

Acknowledgements
The publishers would like to thank the following for
permission to reproduce photographs:

Alamy Images p. **10** (Blickwinkel); FLPA pp. **6**
(Minden Pictures/Frans Lanting), **14** (Minden
Pictures/Frans Lanting), **21** (Martin B. Withers);
Getty Images pp. **11** (The Image Bank), **25** (Gallo
Images), **26** (Digital Vision); Imagestate p. **17**
(Anup Shah); NHPA pp. **4 left** (Andy Rouse),
4 right (Daryl Balfour), **12 bottom** (Ann & Steve
⋯ (Martin Harvey), ⋯ **16** ⋯ (Andy Rouse), **18** (Andy Rouse), **22**
⋯se), **23** (Martin Harvey), **28** (Jonathan
⋯Scott); Photolibrary.com pp. **7**, **9** (Mark
⋯, **15**, **19** (Martyn Colbeck), **29**; Steve
⋯ **8**, **12 top**, **20**, **24**.

J599.   ⋯tograph of a white rhinoceros reproduced
6   ⋯ssion of Naturepl.com/Mark Carwardine.
⋯otograph of an African elephant reproduced
⋯ssion of Steve Bloom.

Every effort has been made to contact copyright
holders of any material reproduced in this book.
Any omissions will be rectified in subsequent
printings if notice is given to the publishers.

The paper used to print this book comes from
sustainable resources.

Disclaimer
All the Internet addresses (URLs) given in this book
were valid at the time of going to press. However,
due to the dynamic nature of the Internet, some
addresses may have changed, or sites may have
changed or ceased to exist since publication. While
the author and publishers regret any inconvenience
this may cause readers, no responsibility for any
such changes can be accepted by either the author
or the publishers.

Contents

Any words appearing in the text in bold, **like this**, are explained in the glossary.

Meet the massive mammals

In the hot afternoon sun, the world's biggest land **mammals roam** across the African plains. A hungry elephant tears branches from a thorny tree with its powerful trunk. Several kilometres away a white rhinoceros stabs its horn into the ground to find roots. Both animals are wary. They sniff the air for signs of danger.

Elephants and rhinos are **herbivores**. They only eat plants. A herbivore's body is designed to help it find food and avoid meat-eating **predators**.

In Kenya, angry African elephants have killed over 200 people in the last seven years.

It would be frightening to meet a white rhino in the wild.

4

There are two types of elephant – Asian and African elephants. African elephants are larger and they roam the grasslands, forests, and deserts of most countries in Africa.

There are five different types of rhino. White and black rhinos are both found in Africa. Black rhinos are known for being very fierce, but white rhinos are bigger and heavier.

White rhinos and African elephants are both strong, tough fighters. But which herbivore would be the champion? Let's find out!

This map shows where African elephants and white rhinos can be found in the wild

NORTH AMERICA

United Kingdom

EUROPE

United States

ATLANTIC OCEAN

AFRICA

ASIA

PACIFIC OCEAN

PACIFIC OCEAN

SOUTH AMERICA

INDIAN OCEAN

AUSTRALIA

N
W   E
S

0   500   1000 Miles
0   500   1000 Kilometres

SOUTHERN   OCEAN

ANTARCTICA

KEY
African elephants
White rhinos
Both elephants and rhinos

5

Size, strength, and brain

ROUND
1

The biggest animals have the best choice of food. Size and strength are also important for attracting **mates**.

Elephant power

African elephants are the largest and heaviest land **mammals** in the world. Male elephants keep growing until they are at least 35 years old!

Their enormous size means that they are able to reach fruit that is high in the treetops. They can even push trees over to get at the juiciest leaves.

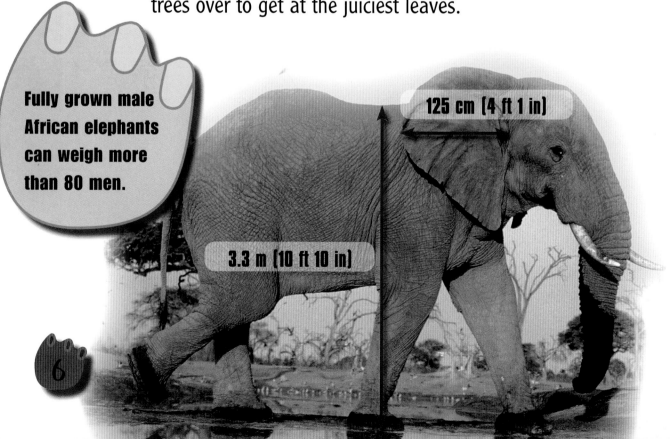

Fully grown male African elephants can weigh more than 80 men.

125 cm (4 ft 1 in)

3.3 m (10 ft 10 in)

Bulky bodies

White rhinos are the world's second largest land animals.
They have a huge hump of muscle on their back, which
they use to move their massive head. Their tough lips
are designed for tearing huge mouthfuls of grass.

Thick skinned

Elephants and rhinos have tough, wrinkly skin. In some
places it is more than 4 centimetres (almost 2 inches)
thick. The bumps and folds help these huge animals
to keep cool, because lots of skin means that a lot
of air and water can reach the animal.

A white rhino's barrel-shaped body is longer than many cars.

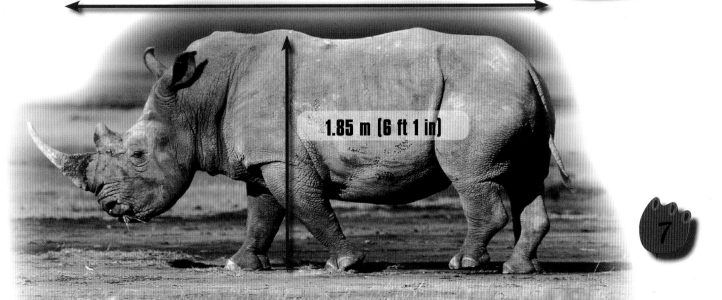

4.2 m (13 ft 9 in)

1.85 m (6 ft 1 in)

7

Size equals strength

Bulky bodies make elephants and rhinos amazingly strong. They don't attack other animals for food, but they can be very dangerous when they are angry or frightened.

Ferocious females

Young elephants and rhinos are small enough to be **prey** for lions and hyenas. Their mothers are always on the lookout for danger.

If a **predator** comes too close, female elephants often **charge** forward with their ears spread and head held high. An attacker that does not move is in danger of getting trampled!

Female rhinos can be very dangerous if their young are in danger.

Big brains

Elephants are very intelligent. They easily remember the best places to find food at different times of the year. They are also very good at learning how to use tools. Some even use branches to swat flies off their skin.

Rhinos cannot solve problems like elephants can, and they spend much less time learning survival skills. But they make up for it with enormous strength and speed.

Elephant trunks are strong enough to lift heavy branches.

WINNER

HEAD TO HEAD	Elephant	Rhino	
Size	10	8	Elephant reaches up to the top prize.
Strength	10	9	Biggest is the best.
Intelligence	10	6	Elephant is definitely not dumbo!

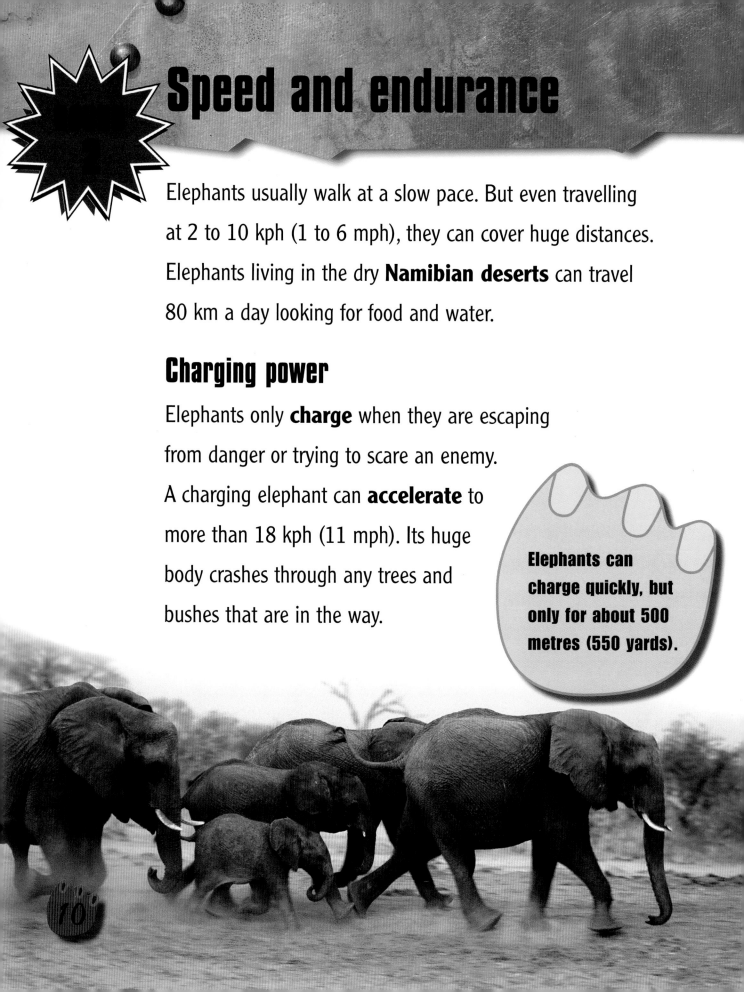

Speed and endurance

Elephants usually walk at a slow pace. But even travelling at 2 to 10 kph (1 to 6 mph), they can cover huge distances. Elephants living in the dry **Namibian deserts** can travel 80 km a day looking for food and water.

Charging power

Elephants only **charge** when they are escaping from danger or trying to scare an enemy. A charging elephant can **accelerate** to more than 18 kph (11 mph). Its huge body crashes through any trees and bushes that are in the way.

Elephants can charge quickly, but only for about 500 metres (550 yards).

Unlike elephants, rhinos do not **roam** over large areas. They only leave their **territory** if they cannot find water there.

Running rhinos

White rhinos look clumsy but it is surprising how fast they can run. Their short, muscular legs are strong enough to support their heavy bodies as they gallop along at 40 kph (25 mph). This is as fast as a galloping horse!

A rhino can also trot at almost 30 kph (19 mph). It can keep moving at this speed for several kilometres without a break.

Rhinos are much faster than they look.

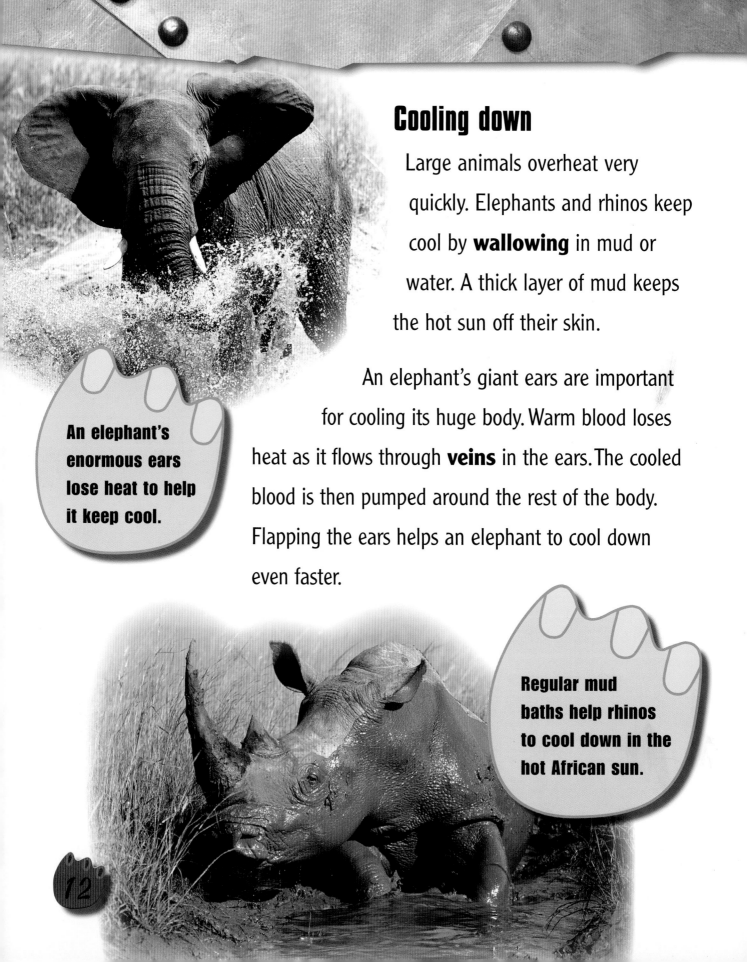

Cooling down

Large animals overheat very quickly. Elephants and rhinos keep cool by **wallowing** in mud or water. A thick layer of mud keeps the hot sun off their skin.

An elephant's giant ears are important for cooling its huge body. Warm blood loses heat as it flows through **veins** in the ears. The cooled blood is then pumped around the rest of the body. Flapping the ears helps an elephant to cool down even faster.

An elephant's enormous ears lose heat to help it keep cool.

Regular mud baths help rhinos to cool down in the hot African sun.

Eating and drinking

Elephants and rhinos can feed at any time of the day or night. Rhinos spend up to half their lives eating or looking for food.

Massive African elephants need to eat up to 200 kg (440 lb) of roots, grasses, leaves, bark, berries, and fruit every day.

Elephants need to drink every day, but white rhinos can last up to four days without water. This helps them to survive **droughts** without leaving their safe **home range**.

A food chain shows who eats what in a habitat.

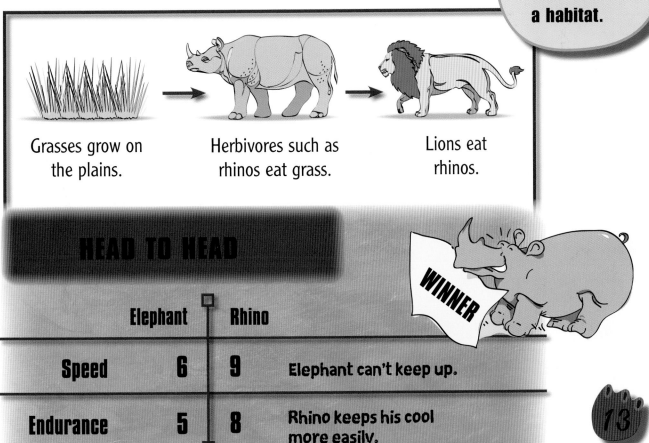

Grasses grow on the plains.

Herbivores such as rhinos eat grass.

Lions eat rhinos.

HEAD TO HEAD

WINNER

	Elephant	Rhino	
Speed	6	9	Elephant can't keep up.
Endurance	5	8	Rhino keeps his cool more easily.

13

Super senses

Sharp **senses** help **herbivores** to find food and mates. They are also important for avoiding enemies.

Short-sighted

Rhinos cannot see very well, but they have a fantastic sense of smell. A rhino's nostrils take up more space than its brain!

Rhinos use smell to detect danger. They can smell an enemy when it is still far away, so the rhino has plenty of time to escape.

Rhinos also have excellent hearing. They twist their ears around to work out where a sound is coming from.

Huge nostrils are a sign that rhinos have a super sense of smell.

14

Smell is also the most important sense for an elephant. Elephants lift their trunks and sniff the air for signs of danger.

Distant danger

Elephants can hear much lower sounds than we can. Their trunks and feet are packed with **receptors** that detect **vibrations** in the ground. They can feel low rumbling sounds made by other elephants 5 kilometres (3 miles) away. Scientists think that elephants use these rumbles to warn each other of danger.

Elephants use their trunks to tell their herd when they are in danger.

15

Super nose!

A trunk does the job of our nose, arms, and hands! An elephant uses its trunk to grab food from the ground or from treetops, and place it in its mouth.

At the end of an African elephant's trunk, there are two finger-like tips that can pick up the tiniest berry or blade of grass. The trunk is not only flexible (easy to move) – it is also strong enough to tear down branches and lift the weight of four men.

Amazing trunks
A trunk can even act as a snorkel when an elephant walks or swims in deep water!

Elephants use their trunks to reach the highest branches of trees.

Trunks are also used to breathe, drink, feel, smell, squirt water, fight, and play.

Elephant's secret weapon

Trunks are excellent weapons. Rival male elephants test each other's strength by twisting their trunks together and pushing or pulling. Angry elephants scare enemies by rolling their trunk up and uncurling it in a sudden swish, while trumpeting loudly. The same movement can be used to throw branches, bones, or rocks.

Rival elephants test each other's strength by locking their trunks together.

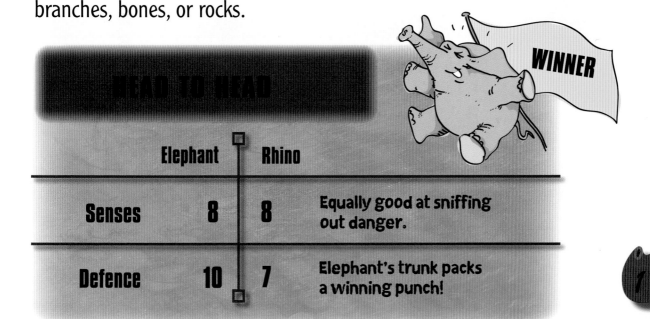

WINNER

HEAD TO HEAD	Elephant	Rhino	
Senses	8	8	Equally good at sniffing out danger.
Defence	10	7	Elephant's trunk packs a winning punch!

17

Deadly weapons

White rhinos have two pointed horns on top of their head. A male's front horn grows up to 1.2 metres (4 feet) long. In very hot weather, rhinos use their horns to dig for water in dry **riverbeds**. They also dig up the soil to find juicy roots when the grass is too short to eat.

Rhino horns are made out of the same material as fingernails and hooves. They wear down easily and can even break off in a fight!

This rhino has been using his horn to dig in the mud.

Tremendous teeth

An elephant's tusks are made of ivory. This is much tougher than rhino horn. Tusks are very long front teeth that keep growing and growing! Some large males have tusks more than 2 metres (6.5 feet) long.

Elephants use their tusks to help them feed. They are tools for shredding bark from trees and digging for roots. Inside the elephant's mouth there are four flat teeth, which are used for grinding food.

Each huge tusk weighs up to 60 kg (130 lb), the weight of two children!

A warning sign

Elephants and rhinos share their African **habitat** with hungry lions and hyenas. Sharp horns and tusks help to keep these **predators** away.

Male elephants and rhinos also use their weapons to threaten other males. An elephant can use its long tusks to stab or wrestle other elephants. Tusks protect the elephant's trunk in a fight.

Male elephants lock tusks and try to tip each other off balance.

Horn wrestling

Young rhinos have wrestling matches with their horns to test their strength. Sometimes these turn into proper fights. One stab with a sharp horn can seriously injure or even kill another rhino.

The size of a rival's horn helps adult rhinos to decide whether to stay and fight, or run away. When males meet, they rub their horns on the ground to show off their size.

Rhino horns usually grow back if they are knocked off in a fight.

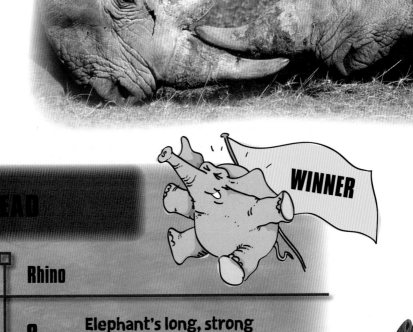

WINNER

	Elephant	Rhino	
HEAD TO HEAD			
Weapons	9	8	Elephant's long, strong tusks are up to the task.

Fighting skills

Rhinos like to live alone in small **territories**. Males let females and smaller males live nearby, but get very angry if they see another large male.

Staring each other out

Rival males never fight straight away. They stare at each other and turn their heads from side to side.

Then they stand nose to nose as each one judges how strong his rival is. Eventually the weaker rhino gives up and runs away, because he does not want to get hurt. Proper fights between rhinos are rare.

A staring match between male rhinos is called "head flagging".

22

Fight for the right to mate

Male elephants don't defend territories. However, they often compete with other males for the right to **mate**. Only the biggest, strongest males can attract females.

When two males meet for the first time they have a mock battle to find out who is most powerful. They wrestle gently with their trunks and tusks until the weaker male backs down.

Elephants have excellent memories. If the same males meet many years later, they will remember who won the first wrestling match and avoid fighting again.

Female elephants work together to protect the babies from predators.

23

Fighting to the death

Sometimes two rival rhinos or elephants are so well matched that a proper fight breaks out.

Fights between male rhinos can be vicious. They swing their heavy heads upwards, trying to stab each other with sharp horns. Both winner and loser might be wounded or even killed.

Male madness

Male elephants fight each other more often. When an adult male is ready to **mate** he becomes very aggressive. This is called **musth** (which means "madness") and it happens to every male once a year.

Male elephants start going into musth when they become adults.

Young rhinos learn fighting skills by playing with their brothers and sisters.

Elephants in musth have a special smell that warns other males to stay away. Only another male in musth would dare to approach. When this happens they may fight to the death.

Learning to fight

Young **mammals** learn how to fight by watching adults. Young elephants practise by pushing each other, banging tusks, and wrestling with heads and trunks.

WINNER

HEAD TO HEAD

	Elephant	Rhino	
Fighting skill	9	9	Practice makes perfect for both beasts.
Aggression	9	7	Must avoid elephants in musth!

Who wins?

Huge powerful bodies, tough skin, and sharp horns or tusks protect adult rhinos and elephants from **predators**.

But what happens when they meet each other in the wild? You've seen the evidence, but can you decide which **herbivore** would be crowned champion?

This elephant is spreading its ears to scare off a rhino.

Armed combat

Male rhinos hate finding intruders in their **territory**. The rhino would try to scare the elephant away by showing his horn and growling. But male elephants are not easily scared! The **mammals** would charge towards each other, trying to stab their rival with a tusk or horn.

White rhinos are tough and speedy. But massive bodies, huge tusks, and a good memory make male elephants almost unbeatable! In South Africa, angry male elephants in **musth** have trampled white rhinos to death. The rhino would be wise to gallop to safety.

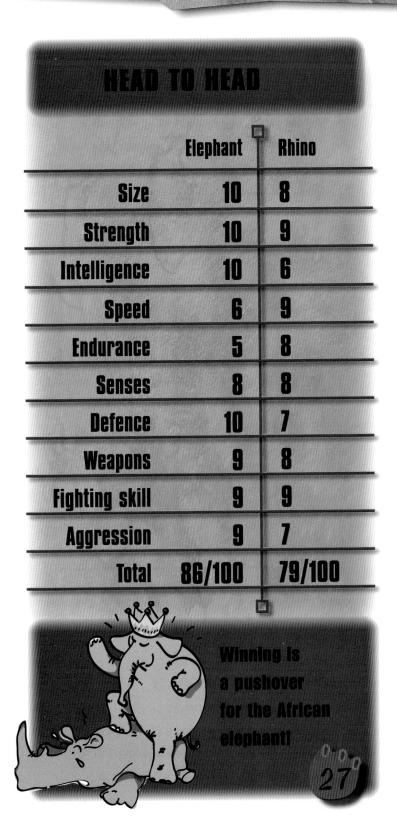

HEAD TO HEAD

	Elephant	Rhino
Size	10	8
Strength	10	9
Intelligence	10	6
Speed	6	9
Endurance	5	8
Senses	8	8
Defence	10	7
Weapons	9	8
Fighting skill	9	9
Aggression	9	7
Total	86/100	79/100

Winning is a pushover for the African elephant!

The real fight

Elephants and rhinos stay away from each other in the wild. But they have a much worse enemy that cannot be avoided – humans.

Habitat loss

Millions of elephants and rhinos once grazed on Africa's grasslands. But people are taking more and more land for houses and farms, so these huge **mammals** have less space to live in, and less food and water.

Millions of elephants and rhinos have been killed for their tusks and horns. Some people believe rhino horn will make them strong. A kilogram of powdered horn can be sold for thousands of pounds.

In the past, elephant ivory was used to make jewellery, piano keys, and tools.

A cruel trade

During the 1980s, 200 elephants were killed for their ivory every day. Buying and selling ivory is now banned. But at least 4,000 elephants are still killed by **poachers** every year. Even the world's biggest animals are no match for a human with a gun.

The future

Most wild elephants and rhinos can only survive in **national parks**, where they are protected from hunters. Unless humans protect the African habitat, these awesome mammals may soon become **extinct**.

Park rangers protect rhinos by sawing their horns off, so that poachers leave them alone.

HOW MANY ARE LEFT?	
African elephant	300,000
White rhino	11,000

29

Glossary

accelerate speed up

charge to attack another animal by running forward

drought very dry weather, when there is not enough rain for plants to grow, or for animals to drink

endurance strength and energy to survive in difficult conditions

extinct when a type of animal does not exist anymore

habitat place where an animal lives

herbivore animal that mainly eats grasses and other plants

home range animal's territory, or the area of land where it looks for food and water

mammal animal that can make its own body heat and produce milk for its babies

mate have babies

mates animals that have babies together

musth period once a year, when adult male elephants are very ferocious and likely to attack

Namibian deserts areas of desert in Namibia, a country in southwest Africa

national park area of land that is protected

poacher person who hunts animals when it is against the law to do so

predator animal that hunts, kills, and eats other animals

prey animal that is caught, killed, and eaten by another animal as food

receptors sensitive cells in an animal's body that can detect certain changes in the surroundings

riverbeds ground at the bottom of a river

roam move over a large area

senses ways in which an animal gets information about its surroundings

territory area that an animal lives in and defends against rivals

vein type of blood vessel that carries blood towards the heart after it has been pumped around the body

vibration quick back and forth movement or shaking

wallowing lying down and rolling around in mud, water, or dust

More information

Books

Animals under threat: Black rhino, Richard and Louise Spilsbury (Heinemann Library, 2004) tells you about another kind of rhinoceros and how humans have put them in danger.

Life in a herd: Elephants, Richard and Louise Spilsbury (Heinemann Library, 2004) looks at how elephants behave when they are in a group.

Why am I a mammal?, Greg Pyers (Raintree, 2005) will tell you more about elephant and rhino biology.

Websites

www.nationalgeographic.com/kids – visit this site and click on "Creature Features" to find lots of great photos and facts.

www.bbc.co.uk/reallywild – this site is packed with facts, features, and games to help you find out all about the world's most amazing creatures. You can even play a recording of an elephant trumpeting!

http://www.panda.org – this is the website of the World Wildlife Fund, which is working to save animals and their habitats around the world. Go to "education" and then "middle school" to find out more about elephants, rhinos, and other endangered creatures.

Sizing up the elephant and rhinoceros

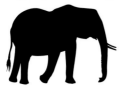 

This picture shows how big an African elephant and a white rhino are.

Index

Titles in the *Animals Head to Head* series include:

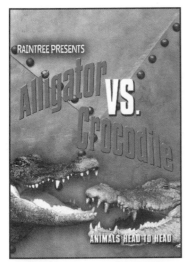

Hardback   1 406 20331 9

Hardback   1 406 20329 7

Hardback   1 406 20327 0

Hardback   1 406 20330 0

Hardback   1 406 20332 7

Hardback   1 406 20328 9

Find out about the other titles in this series on our website www.raintreepublishers.co.uk